AFRICAN WILD DOG PACK VS. LEOPARD

BY NATHAN SOMMER

BELLWETHER MEDIA • MINNEAPOLIS, MN

Torque brims with excitement
perfect for thrill-seekers of all kinds.
Discover daring survival skills, explore
uncharted worlds, and marvel at mighty
engines and extreme sports. In *Torque* books,
anything can happen. Are you ready?

This edition first published in 2024 by Bellwether Media, Inc.

No part of this publication may be reproduced in whole or in part without written
permission of the publisher. For information regarding permission, write to
Bellwether Media, Inc., Attention: Permissions Department,
6012 Blue Circle Drive, Minnetonka, MN 55343.

Library of Congress Cataloging-in-Publication Data

LC record for African Wild Dog Pack vs. Leopard available at:
https://lccn.loc.gov/2023045269

Text copyright © 2024 by Bellwether Media, Inc. TORQUE and associated logos are
trademarks and/or registered trademarks of Bellwether Media, Inc.

Editor: Suzane Nguyen   Designer: Josh Brink

Printed in the United States of America, North Mankato, MN.

TABLE OF CONTENTS

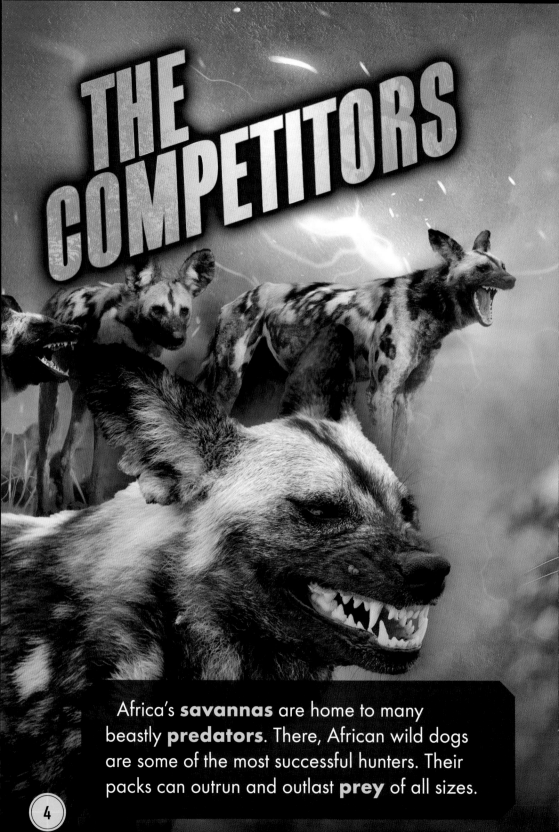

THE COMPETITORS

Africa's **savannas** are home to many beastly **predators**. There, African wild dogs are some of the most successful hunters. Their packs can outrun and outlast **prey** of all sizes.

The dogs meet their match in leopards. These **agile** wild cats are dangerous on the ground and in the trees. Who wins a battle between these two predators?

African wild dogs have long legs, bushy tails, and large, rounded ears. Their short, patchy coats are mostly yellow, black, and white.

African wild dogs are very social animals. They live in large groups called packs. These groups can be found in the grasslands, woodlands, and deserts of **sub-Saharan** Africa.

SPECIAL COATS

No two African wild dogs have the same coat. Each of their coats have different patterns.

AFRICAN WILD DOG PROFILE

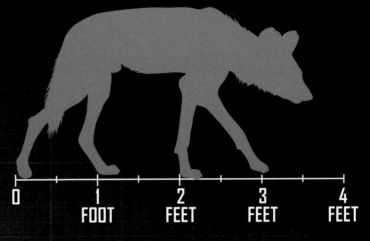

```
├────┼────┼────┼────┼────┼────┼────┼────┤
0         1         2         3         4
        FOOT      FEET      FEET      FEET
```

LENGTH
UP TO 3.6 FEET
(1.1 METERS)

WEIGHT
UP TO 79 POUNDS
(36 KILOGRAMS)

HABITAT

GRASSLANDS   WOODLANDS   DESERTS

AFRICAN WILD DOG RANGE

■ RANGE

LEOPARD PROFILE

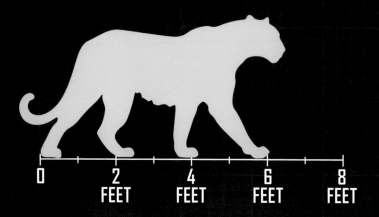

```
0        2        4        6        8
FEET     FEET     FEET     FEET
```

LENGTH
AROUND 6.2 FEET
(1.9 METERS)

WEIGHT
UP TO 165 POUNDS
(75 KILOGRAMS)

HABITAT

RAIN FORESTS   GRASSLANDS   DESERTS   MOUNTAINS

LEOPARD RANGE

■ RANGE

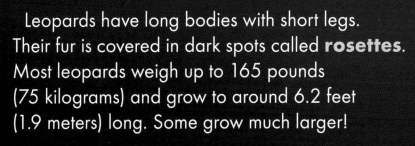

Leopards have long bodies with short legs. Their fur is covered in dark spots called **rosettes**. Most leopards weigh up to 165 pounds (75 kilograms) and grow to around 6.2 feet (1.9 meters) long. Some grow much larger!

Leopards are **solitary** animals. They roam throughout the grasslands, deserts, and mountains of Asia and Africa.

ROSETTES

STAY OUT!

Leopards guard their home areas. They spray urine and scratch trees to warn other leopards to stay away.

SECRET WEAPONS

African wild dogs usually hunt in packs of 5 to 20 dogs. Some packs can have 40 dogs! The dogs talk using quiet, bird-like whines and yelps. This teamwork helps them defeat much larger prey.

FOUR-TOED HUNTERS

African wild dogs are the only dogs that have four toes on each foot.

LEOPARD CLAW

1 INCH
(2.5 CENTIMETERS)

Leopards have sharp claws. They use them to hold onto prey. The claws can be up to 1 inch (2.5 centimeters) long.

TOP SPEED

44 MILES (71 KILOMETERS) PER HOUR
AFRICAN WILD DOG

28 MILES (45 KILOMETERS) PER HOUR
FASTEST HUMAN

African wild dogs are incredible runners. Long legs help them reach speeds of up to 44 miles (71 kilometers) per hour. Large lungs help them chase prey for 3 miles (5 kilometers) without slowing down!

Leopards have powerful legs. This helps them run in bursts of up to 36 miles (58 kilometers) per hour. They can also leap up to 20 feet (6 meters) forward!

SECRET WEAPONS

PACKS

LONG LEGS

LARGE EARS

African wild dogs have great hearing.
Their large, rounded ears can find faraway prey.
The dogs raise or lower their ears to
communicate while hunting.

SECRET WEAPONS

SHARP CLAWS

POWERFUL LEGS

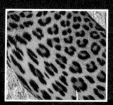

ROSETTES

Leopards use their rosettes as **camouflage**. This makes them hard to see in thick grass or on tree branches. The cats can catch prey by surprise.

ATTACK MOVES

African wild dogs eat whatever they can catch.
Packs quietly approach prey. Then they chase it
for long distances until the prey gets tired.

Leopards are **stealthy** hunters. They **stalk** prey. They may also sit on tree branches to wait for prey to come close. Then they pounce in a surprise attack!

NIGHT VISION

Leopards can see in the dark seven times better than humans can.

African wild dog packs circle their tired prey. They move in as a group. They attack with painful bites. Meals are then shared among the pack.

After pouncing, leopards attack prey using their sharp claws. They defeat their meals with bites to the neck. Leopards often store their prey up in trees to hide it from other predators.

READY, FIGHT!

An African wild dog spots a leopard. It yelps to prepare pack members for a group battle. The leopard sees the pack coming close. A chase begins!

Pack members bite the leopard during the chase. The leopard uses its sharp claws to scratch the dogs. Then it climbs a tree to quickly escape. The wild cat outsmarted the dogs today!

GLOSSARY

agile—able to move quickly and easily

camouflage—colors and patterns that help an animal hide in its surroundings

communicate—to share thoughts and feelings using sounds, faces, and actions

predators—animals that hunt other animals for food

prey—animals that are hunted by other animals for food

rosettes—the spots on a leopard

savannas—flat grasslands in Africa with very few trees

solitary—related to living alone

stalk—to follow closely and quietly

stealthy—to be secretive or unnoticed

sub-Saharan—the area in Africa that is south of the Sahara Desert

TO LEARN MORE

AT THE LIBRARY

Hudak, Heather. *Wolf, Coyote, and Other Packs*. New York, N.Y.: Crabtree Publishing, 2023.

Sommer, Nathan. *Gorilla vs. Leopard*. Minneapolis, Minn.: Bellwether Media, 2020.

Winter, Steve, and Sharon Guynup. *The Ultimate Book of Big Cats*. Washington D.C.: National Geographic Kids, 2022.

ON THE WEB

FACTSURFER

Factsurfer.com gives you a safe, fun way to find more information.

1. Go to www.factsurfer.com

2. Enter "African wild dog pack vs. leopard" into the search box and click 🔍.

3. Select your book cover to see a list of related content.

INDEX

The images in this book are reproduced through the courtesy of: Johan Swanepoel, cover (African wild dog); Volodymyr Burdiak, cover (leopard); Thomas Retterath, pp. 2-3, 20-21, 22-24 (blur dogs); Henk Bogaard, pp. 2-3, 20-21, 22-24 (foreground focused dogs); Zoonar/ kavram/ Alamy, pp. 2-3, 20-21, 22-24 (leopard); Ikpro, pp. 2-3, 20-21, 22-24 (tree stump); Wandering views, p. 4 (wild dog foreground); paula french, p. 4 (wild dogs background); Sergey Uryadnikov, p. 5 (leopard); Roby1960, pp. 6-7; jeep2499, pp. 8-9 (main photo, call out); Siempreverde22, p. 10; Costa Frangeskides, p. 11; imageBROKER/ Shem Compion/ Alamy, p. 12; Elana Erasmus, p. 13; Cheryl Jayaratne, p. 14; Diressh Parbhoo, p. 14 (packs); Ondrej Prosicky, p. 14 (long legs, large ears); Mike Powles/ Getty Images, p. 15; Londolozi Images/ Mint Images/ Getty, p. 15 (sharp claws); kavram, p. 15 (powerful legs, rosettes); Ondrej Prosicky/ Getty Images, p. 16; Anders Stoustrup, p. 17; BRUCE DAVIDSON/ Alamy, p. 18; Thomas Stanton, p. 19.